A Parent's Heart

Ivelize Vega

Presentation by *BookLeaf Publishing*

Web: www.bookleafpub.com

E-mail: info@bookleafpub.com

ISBN: 9789357742368

First edition 2023

I dedicate this book to my two daughters Isabel and Ava. They taught me the real meaning of unconditional love and being their mom is my greatest joy.

Love In Gold

Bursting heart at birth
A parent's love is golden
Rich, pure and treasured

A Mother's Guide

There's no guidebook in being a mother,
especially since each child is different from another.
All we can do is ask God for guidance,
in hopes that our prayers will be answered in abundance.

A Parent's Worry

I worried when I was pregnant that my baby
would be born too early and be weak.
I worried when she was a baby that she
would stop breathing in her sleep.
I worried when she started walking that she
would lose her balance and fall into a creek.
I worried when she went to preschool that she
would get lost while playing hide-and-seek.
I worried when she was in elementary school that she
would be too shy and not speak.
I worried when she was in middle school that she
wouldn't be able to turn the other cheek.
I worried when she entered high school that she
wouldn't be able to maintain her good academic streak.

Emotions

When they cry, I cry
When they hurt, I hurt
When they smile, I smile
When they laugh, I laugh

As She Flips

I see her working to achieve her dream,
as she carefully flips off the beam.
Running fast towards the vault,
in an effort not to halt.

She flips herself over the bar,
moving like a shooting star.
She stretches immensely to hit the floor,
then waits patiently for her final score.

A Parent's Form

You can be a Single parent,
Divorced or Widowed parent,
Working or Stay at home parent,
Caucasian or Asian parent,
Black, Brown or Hispanic parent.

But at the end of the day you're still just like any other parent,
Working hard in your child's life to remain just as apparent.

A Parent's Role

To be a child's caretaker is to be a parent
it's motivating your child even when you aren't
and raising them to be an adult that pays their own rent.

A Parent's Night

I remember falling asleep when you were a baby in my belly,
then you were born so I'd wake up to change diapers when they were smelly.

I remember watching you sleep as an infant,
and wondering if you would grow up to be brilliant.

I remember reading you a bedtime story when you were nine,
but now you're older and put yourself to bed so I just drink a glass of wine.

In This World

In this world you are seen as brown,
therefore I want you to walk around like you have a crown.
Just remember you are more than the color of your skin,
so be sure to always hold up your chin.

In this world you should be strong,
because at times society may make will you feel wrong.
Just remember you will always have a place,
for the world needs to know your beautiful face.

I Am Not

I am not your little friend
although I enjoy hearing about your day.
I am not your maid
although I enjoy having a clean house everyday.
I am not your personal cook
although I want to make sure you eat well all-day.
I am not your personal chauffeur
although I want to make sure you get to places with no delay.
I am not your ATM machine
although I want to make sure you have money to always pay.

Work

I don't work because I enjoy it,
I work so you can have clothes that fit.

I don't work for pleasure,
I work so we have a home that you can treasure.

I don't work for fun,
I work so you can go to the beach and lay in the sun.

Co-Parents

I may not have stayed married to your dad,
but I do not want you to be sad,
because I'm grateful for the time together that we had.

We were childhood sweethearts that fell in love,
but things got tough so we grew apart thereof,
although we're no longer together we'll work to co-parent hand in glove.

When You Were Younger

When you were younger, you'd get home and sit on my lap
but now that you're older, you get home and fade into a nap.

When you were younger, you'd play outside with a ball
but now that you're older, you just want to go to the mall.

When you were younger, you'd let me pick out your clothes
but now that you're older, you study the outfits that I pick and find loathes.

When you were younger, you'd wear a big flower headband
but now that you're older, you occasionally just wear a Nike wristband.

When you were younger, I couldn't wait for you to grow up fast
but now that you're older, I keep looking back at the past.

I Hope

I hope you continue to embrace your beautiful curly hair,
even if it feels like people continue to stare,
just know it's because they can't compare,
to someone that has such great flair.

I May Not Be

I may not be a good cook,
but I can follow recipes in a book.

I may not be a mathematician,
but I can help you with basic addition.

I may not be a seamstress,
but I can help you find a nice dress.

My Sun

My girls are my sun,
they make me smile everyday,
and brighten my days.

Complete Love

I love you completely unconditionally everyday.
I love you completely unconditionally.
I love you completely.
I love you.

As You Grow Up

As you grow up, I want you to be humble
and to always pick yourself up after you stumble.

As you grow up, I want you to spread kindness
and to always treat people with politeness.

As you grow up, I want you to be smart
and to always act with a caring heart.

Printed in the USA
CPSIA information can be obtained
at www.ICGtesting.com
LVHW010440120224
771308LV00016B/1399